MALVERN 1600-1800

MALVERN 1600-1800

View of Great Malvern from Mr. Savage's orchard, 1744 (Malvern Museum)

Paul Backhouse

Malvern 1600–1800
Paul Backhouse

Published by Greyhound Self-Publishing 2017
Malvern, Worcestershire, United Kingdom.

Printed and bound by Aspect Design
89 Newtown Road, Malvern, Worcs. WR14 1PD
United Kingdom
Tel: 01684 561567
E-mail: allan@aspect-design.net
Website: www.aspect-design.net

All Rights Reserved.

Copyright © 2017 Paul Backhouse

Paul Backhouse has asserted his moral right
to be identified as the author of this work.

The right of Paul Backhouse to be identified as the author
of this work has been asserted in accordance with
Section 77 of the Copyright, Designs and Patents Act 1988.

This book is sold subject to the condition that it shall not, by way of trade
or otherwise, be lent, resold, hired out or otherwise circulated without
the publisher's prior consent in any form of binding or cover other than
that in which it is published and without a similar condition including
this condition being imposed on the subsequent purchaser.

ISBN 978-1-909219-36-6

Preface

This book covers the history of Malvern from the year 1600 to around 1800, stopping before the rapid growth of Great Malvern as a spa town in the 19th century. The history follows on from my two earlier books on Medieval Malvern and on Tudor Malvern.

The most complete local history for this period is "A History of Malvern" by Brian S Smith, which is complemented by "The Forest and Chase of Malvern" by Pamela Hurle, which includes copies of the map showing the enclosure of the Chase in 1633 and the invaluable estate maps of the manor of Great Malvern drawn in 1744.

This book adds considerable detail on the farms and families of Cowleigh and Upper Howsell to the north of the Link, which now lie in Malvern. This is an area that I have been researching for over 15 years. However the detailed history of Baldenhall and Barnards Green presented here is relatively new to me, and I acknowledge the able assistance of Faith Renger in checking my account and in challenging my conclusions.

Paul Backhouse, August 2017

Silver shillings (12 pence) of Elizabeth (1595) James I and Charles I

1   Overview 1600-1800

This book takes Malvern from the year 1600 to around the end of the 18th century. This period includes the Disafforestation of Malvern Chase with the enclosure and sale of land by Charles I, the English Civil War, the recognition of the Malvern Hills as a fashionable place to 'take the water', and later (in the 18th century) the development of improved agricultural practices and the enclosure of common land on the Link. The story ends just as the Industrial Revolution was beginning to take hold in the Midlands, but before the first phase of spa buildings in Great Malvern (starting in the Regency period).

The recorded history of Medieval and Tudor Malvern is largely concerned with the estates of Great Malvern Priory and the manors and estates created after the Dissolution of the Monasteries. In 1600 the principal manors and estates in the immediate area were as follows:

- Great Malvern, and the manor of Powick owned by Henry Bromley of Holt in Worcestershire,
- Madresfield owned by the Lygon family,
- Blackmore Park owned by the Hornyold family, lords of the manor of Hanley Castle,
- Severn End in Hanley Castle owned by the Lechmere family, later also the owners of Cowley Park,
- Abbey House in Great Malvern owned by the Savage family,
- The former priory granges of Newland, and of Guarlford Court and Moat Court in Great Malvern,
- The manor of Leigh owned by the Colles family in 1600, by Sir Walter Devereux from 1615, and later in the 18th century by the Somers-Cocks family of Eastnor Castle.

The Victoria County History volumes for Worcestershire give a detailed account of the descent of these manors. It also covers political, military, trade and industrial history (in volume 2) noting that Sir Henry Bromley was involved in Essex's rebellion against Queen Elizabeth in February 1601. His estates were forfeited to the Crown and only restored by James I.

Otherwise the principal local histories for this period are "A History of Malvern" by Brian S Smith and "The Forest and Chase of Malvern" by Pamela Hurle, which includes copies of the invaluable estate maps of the manor of Great Malvern drawn in 1744 after the purchase of the manor by the Foley family.

The wealth of records available for this period (including property deeds, and wills and inventories) mean that we can also follow the story of individual farms and farmers: the small-holders and tenant farmers as well as the larger leasehold and freehold properties. A number of farms emerge from the manorial system as new freehold properties during the period, including for example Gritt Farm in Howsell, purchased from the manor of Leigh in 1662.

The development of farming practices through this period can be followed in Gaut ("A History of Worcestershire Agriculture") with the position at the beginning of the 19th century described by Pitt ("General View of the Agriculture of the County of Worcester [1813]"). The Agricultural Revolution of the 18th century led to the selective breeding of bigger and better livestock, the use of better crop rotations, and the move towards the enclosure of the old ridge-and-furrow arable fields and common pastures into consolidated fields and smallholdings which were more profitable. Unfortunately the lower class of peasants lost out in this process, often losing their rights of common.

Agricultural specialities in Worcestershire included the growth of tobacco (in the early 17th century, later banned) plus apples and hops, the latter often harvested by a seasonal influx of Welshmen (c.1800, see Pitt). A number of hop fields are identified on the local tithe maps (1830s - 40s). A more unusual crop was flax, used in the manufacture of ropes, needed in rigging for the Royal Navy. Parliament introduced a bounty of 4 pence per stone to encourage its growth. William Harwood of Leigh claimed the flax bounty at the Worcester Quarter Sessions in 1785. He was perhaps the Mr. Harwood who was the tenant at Pale Farm in 1781 (Land Tax).

The church was supported by the system of tithe payments. Tithes were originally paid in kind, to the owner of the rectory, not always the parson (or rector). In Malvern a vicar was employed and only received the 'small tithes' and not the income from the more valuable cereal crops. The tithe was typically one tenth of the parishioners' agricultural produce (for both crops and animals). Sometimes payment in kind was replaced by a money payment (or 'modus') for example for the work of the two mills in Great Malvern (see the list of the parish tithes in 1714 in Nott). Every occupier of lands in Leigh paid a modus of two pence yearly called 'Leighton money' in place of a tithe on fruit paid in kind. This was very favourable to the parishioners in the latter 17th century, and the Rev. Portman tried to get the modus to lapse, so that he could collect the tithe in kind. The payment of Leighton money was upheld in the Lent assizes of 7 Wm III (1695, see Gaut). Other modus payments in Leigh included 'smoke penny' in lieu of all tithe wood, 'garden penny' in lieu of "all tythable matters growing in the garden", one penny for the tithe milk of each cow, and four pence for a pigeon house. Tithe payments varied from parish to parish. In Great Malvern there were identical payments for smoke penny, for garden penny and for milk, but no modus for pigeons, and significantly "the tenth of cherries and all other marketable fruit whether apples, pears or plums is due at the tree when gathered". All payments in kind were converted into cash payments charged on land in the Tithe Commutation Acts of the 1830s – 40s.

Cloth manufacture was the principal industry in Worcester at the beginning of the 17th century. Some of the wealthier clothiers moved out of the city and bought up country estates, like Rowland Berkeley who purchased the manor of Spetchley and also Cowley, near Malvern. Many later drapers and mercers can be identified by the trade tokens that they issued in the 1650s and 1660s, when there was a shortage of low-value coin. The cloth industry later fell into decline, and leather glove manufacture grew to become the principal trade in Worcester at the end of the 18th century. By 1802 there were 70 glove-masters employing 6,000 hands (see VCH volume 2).

The county was run by the Justices of the Peace, the wealthy 'Squirearchy' of country gentleman, such as Sir Henry Bromley or Sir Walter Devereux (in the 17th century) or the Lygon and Somers-Cocks families (in the 18th). They can be seen in action as magistrates in the Quarter Sessions Rolls, published for

Worcestershire starting the 1590s. It was the Squirearchy who had the right to hunt game and shoot game birds, with increasingly harsh penalties for poachers. In fact the Game Laws enacted by the 'Cavalier Parliament' in 1671 also prevented any freeholders owning land valued at under £100 per year from killing game, even on their own land (the penalty was a £5 fine, or three months imprisonment). So for example, even though he was one of the richest freeholders in the parish of Leigh, Francis Morton of Pale Farm (d.1714) who owned about 60 acres would have been unable to hunt on his own land, which had an annual value of only £29 (later Land Tax Assessment of 1781) even counting his father's property in Eastnor (worth another £40 in 1663). This may explain why his nephew, another Francis Morton (a later owner of Pale Farm) was on the register of deputations to gamekeepers for the manor of Bourton on the Hill and Moreton in Marsh in Gloucestershire in the 1740s, owned by his brother-in-law Robert Bateson, where he could legitimately shoot (Gloucester Record Office).

At the bottom of the social scale, the poorest had to make a living from their labour in the farmer's fields and the produce from their cottage gardens. They could not legitimately take even a rabbit, pigeon or duck. Agricultural wages at the end of the 18th century were low, typically only a shilling (12 pence) per day for a man and 6 pence per day for a woman (in 1794, see Pitt) although more might be earned at harvest time. Those who were too old or infirm to support themselves had to be supported by the charity of the parish of their birth, whose responsibilities were defined by statute. The burden on the parish increased markedly through the 18th century (see "A History of Malvern"). The alms house shown on the 1744 map of Malvern (on modern Church Street) was most likely a parish provision, rather than a medieval survival. Brian Smith records that the parish overseers of the poor later possessed a timber-framed farmhouse at the lower end of Barnards Green, used as a workhouse, but then purchased a 20 acre site at Link Top where a new workhouse was built after 1802. This poor house is shown on the Foley estate map of 1831 (Malvern Museum).

The parish was also responsible for the upkeep of the roads, which were often in a poor state of repair. This typically meant a couple of days labour from each of the parishioners every year, repairing the roads. The road system was improved starting in the early 18th century by the establishment of local turn-pike trusts which maintained the major routes, funded by tolls paid by the road users. By the end of the century there were turnpikes from Worcester to Hereford, between Powick and Upton, and through Powick and the Link to Great Malvern and onwards towards Ledbury. The routes can be identified on the first edition OS map (surveyed in 1817) where the toll-houses are marked (as "T.P."). Coach transport was still in its infancy, and the first coaches from London ran only as far as Worcester, but in May 1758 the postal service was extended to Great Malvern providing the "first regular link with the outside world" (see "A History of Malvern").

The first county maps, the first road maps and the first estate maps come from this period. The documentary evidence includes manorial records as before, but also parish registers, wills and inventories, property deeds, Quarter Sessions records and Hearth Tax and Land Tax assessments. The later tithe maps (1830s-1840s) and Foley estate maps (1831) allow us to map the 18th century farms in more detail.

Amongst the earlier 17th century records are the Hearth Tax returns for Worcestershire, copied onto microfilm at the Worcester Record Office. As an example, the return for Leigh of 1663 records a total of 164 taxable hearths including the 8 of Robert Martin Esq. (at Leigh Court), with 24 in the tything of Upper Howsell and only 12 in Lower Howsell. In Upper Howsell, the following people were assessed for the most hearths:

- Anthony Barnes (3), probably the Anthony 'Baron' of Cowley recorded in the Great Malvern parish registers in 1667, tenant at Cowley Park
- William Barkley (3), perhaps the churchwarden of Great Malvern Priory named in 1665
- Richard Morton (2), of Gritt Farm

In Great Malvern there were 10 taxable hearths for the Savage family (at Abbey House). As an aside, it is interesting to note the numbers of residents of Upper Howsell who appear in the Great Malvern parish registers. The priory church was their closest place of worship, and Francis Morton of Pale Farm was even buried there in 1714 (his grave marker is in the north aisle).

Apart from the early county maps, which contain little detail, one of the earliest useful maps is Ogilby's strip map of the old road from Hereford to Leicester (1675) which skirts the top of modern Malvern and crosses the Teme at Bransford. The local section of a later copy is shown below.

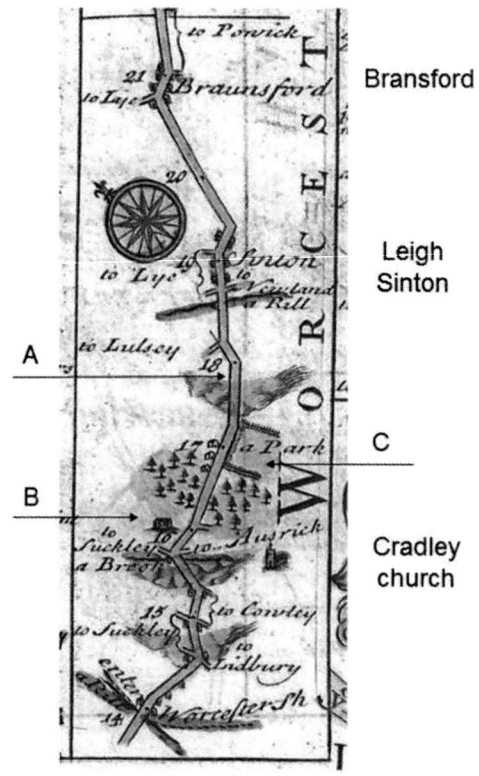

Key:
A is a section of the road along Dragons Lane and Crumpton Hill Lane, now within the boundaries of Malvern Town.

B is shown as the house of 'Mr Sands' on the original map, identified as Martin Sandys of Cradley, gent. (1670s) "late receiver of Hearth-money and of 18 months tax for Co. Worcester" (1678).

C is a deer park on Crumpton Hill (belonging to Sir Robert Berkeley, emparked in 1625).

Note that Cowley, Newland, Suckley and Alfrick are all signposted, but there is no mention of Malvern.

Section of road map (J.Owen and E. Bowen, early 18th century)

The map in the book by the Rev. Thomas (1725) shown on the next page, gives a panoramic view of the Malverns (looking west). Note the Hereford Road (the new turnpike ran to the north of the old road), the Malverne Road through Newland and the Link, and 'Robinson Street' south of Malvern (surely 'Robertsend Street' at Hanley Swan, on the 1st Edition OS map, but actually on the other side of Blackmore Park), and 'Picksham' ferry over the Severn. Also shown are the two beacon towers on the Herefordshire and Worcestershire Beacons, "St Michael's chapel" on the hill in Great Malverne, and the site of the Battle of Worcester (1651) outside St Johns.

The Malvern area in 1725.

2 Malvern Chase – Disafforestation and Inclosure

Charles I attempted to rule England without Parliament. This meant that he could not go to Parliament for money, but had to exploit unpopular sources of funding such as 'Ship Money' and sell off a number Crown rights and properties. It was in this climate that he decided on the Disafforestation of

Malvern Chase, giving up his forest rights in exchange for the enclosure of one third of the Chase for the Crown, which he then sold to the highest bidder. A map of 1633 in the Berrington collection (Worcester Record Office) shows the proposed enclosures across the Chase (the map is reproduced in Pamela Hurle's book, and a copy is on display at Malvern Museum).

King Charles granted his third of the Chase to Sir Cornelius Vermuyden, and the property later passed to Sir George Strode (1637) and was re-granted to his son Sir Nicholas Strode in the 1660s, when the Disafforestation was confirmed by Act of Parliament (1664). The lands descended through the family to the Lyttons, who sold to the Hornyolds of Blackmore Park in 1768.

Of particular relevance to Malvern are the enclosures across North Hill and on the Link Common. Some of the original plots can be traced by the prominent boundary ditches on the hill, or from the boundaries of later farms on the tithe maps. A comment in a survey of the Hornyold estate, dating from about 1768 (Worcester Record Office) notes that "the waste land that was divided out and ditched out at the time of discharging the Chase but lying on the Hills has never been enclosed", effectively dating the surviving boundary ditches to the mid-17th century.

Three plots were enclosed for the Crown on the Link: 60 acres at 'Hauxmore' (later Brick Farm) and the future Jamaica and Moors Farms further down the Link. Sir Walter Devereux, lord of the manor of Leigh, was granted the remaining part of the Link that lay in the parish. He also owned the manor of Cowley where he had been given permission to create a deer park in 1625.

The drawing below gives an interpretation of the enclosures on North Hill and at 'Hauxmore', with boundaries traced from the later OS map. Some of the original text is shown (in serif font) and additional text has been added (in sans-serif font) to help identify the location of modern roads and features. The 'Headway' is the modern Worcester Road, the 'Whore Stone' at Link Top was later moved down to Malvern Link and is now in the church-yard at St. Matthias, and 'Cowley Gate' is at the point where Old Hollow meets the Cowleigh Road, on the old county boundary, and not at Cowleigh Gate Farm.

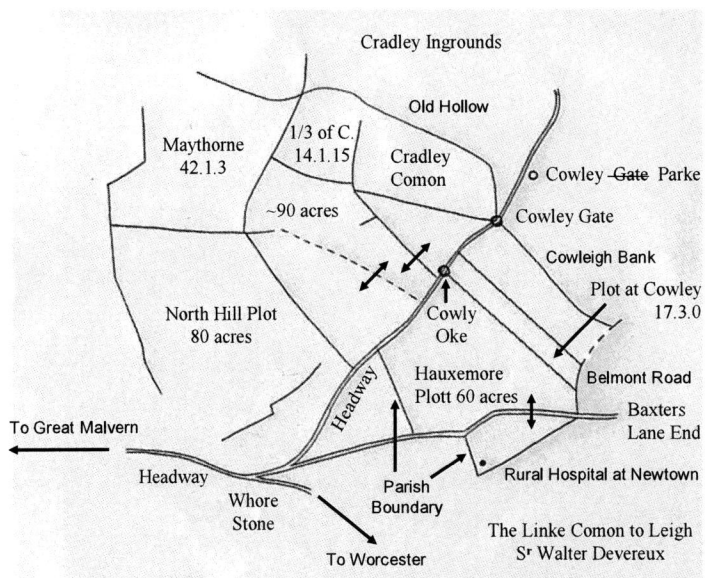

Map of the Chase, 1633 showing enclosures at North Hill (west at the top)

The North Hill and 'Maythorne' (i.e. Mathon) plots are still well delineated by ditches on the hills, as is Cradley Common. Between them, and now disrupted by quarrying (on the former Hornyold lands) is an area of about 90 acres containing (working from the west) a triangle of common land shared by Cradley and Leigh, a strip of "thirds' land", another triangle of common land shared by Leigh and Great Malvern, and another strip of "thirds' land".

Elsewhere, the map of 1633 provides additional information on local families. Besides the land in Great Malvern enclosed for Thomas Bromley, and Redmore Meadow owned by Mr. Savage, we find "Thomas Winsmore his freehold" in the Pickersley area, and "Mr Barnes' Riding" in Poolbrook. To the north of the Link are "Baxters Lane End" and "Mourtons Lane", in Leigh. The Winsmores were a well-established family in Leigh and Newland, and the will of Anthony Barnes gent. of St Johns Bedwardine dated 1653 is available at the National Archives. Baxters Lane End is in the vicinity of the Tanhouse in Upper Howsell (owned by the Baxter family) and Mourtons Lane would have led to the Gritt, farmed by the Morton family.

3   The English Civil War

There was no regular army in England at the outbreak of the English Civil War. England was defended by a militia system, with local 'Trained Bands' raised in the counties and cities. Thus, in 1641 the residents of Malverne Magna, Madresfield and Newland were collectively responsible for providing three pikemen (equipped with 'corslett' (i.e. armour) and pike) and five musketeers for the Worcestershire Trained Band. As part of this assessment, Anthony Barnes, William Knight (of Northend), Rowland Jefford (surely Rowland Gifford, of Moat Court) and Richard Webb were together responsible for equipping Philipp Greene as a pikeman, and Richard Reade and John Warner (of Baldenhall) were responsible for arming Thomas Dipper, a musketeer. The residents of Leigh and Mathon were responsible for arming another four pikemen and four musketeers (see Atkin).

There were also a number of former soldiers and mercenary captains who had served in the Thirty Years War. One notable example was Sir Walter Devereux of Leigh Court, lord of the manor of Leigh. It is quite possible that he was the English captain, named as Walter Devereux who was responsible for the assassination of the famous Austrian general Wallenstein in 1634. A supporter of the Parliamentary cause, at the outset of the English Civil War (1642) Devereux had stockpiled one barrel of powder and 50lbs of match (see Atkin). Although too old to take an active part in the conflict, his eldest son Leicester Devereux, later Viscount Hereford, commanded a regiment of horse. William Lygon and Nicholas Lechmere were also notable Parliamentarians, while Thomas Savage of Elmley Castle and Great Malvern was a Royalist officer and raised a troop of cavalrymen.

The first engagement of the Civil War was Prince Rupert's cavalry action at Powick in 1642. At the end of the first Civil War, Madresfield Court and the city of Worcester were besieged and taken by Parliament in 1646. Worcester was also the site of Cromwell's victory over Charles II and his Scottish allies in 1651, now commemorated at the Commandery museum in Worcester.

Towards the end of the first Civil War, local people adopted a position of armed neutrality in associations of 'Clubmen', designed to defend law and order, and in February 1645 a thousand Worcestershire Clubmen prevented three troops of Royalist horse from plundering the home of Sir Walter Devereux at Leigh Court (see Atkin). Gradually the Clubmen militia distanced itself from the Royalist cause, and in 1646 they participated in the Parliamentarian sieges of Madresfield and Worcester. Among the Royalist gentry captured at the siege of Worcester were Henry Bromley of Holt, Thomas Hornyold of Blackmore Park and William Langston of Hanley (Castle).

At the end of the war, Sir Walter Devereux petitioned parliament for compensation for damages suffered to his properties in Leigh, including (it has been suggested) the destruction of his manor-house at Cowley Park. Meanwhile, the former Royalist, Thomas Savage was fined £1,500 despite losses to his crops and buildings worth £600 (see VCH, Elmley Castle).

Cromwell and his major-generals ruled England during the 1650s. Former Royalists were fined ('compounded') or had their property seized until the fine could be paid. The Calendar of the Committee for Compounding from February 1655 records a case concerning a messuage in 'Upper Howsill' (probably Pale Farm) which William Morton had demised (leased) to Robert Ridley. It was claimed that the County Committee had wrongly distrained Ridley's cattle on the pretence that the land-owner, William Morton was a recusant (i.e. a Catholic).

Leicester Devereux, Viscount Hereford, was one of six peers who invited Charles II to return to England in 1660. The militia system continued after the Restoration, and Worcestershire had two troops of 60 horse and a regiment of 786 foot in the 1690s (see VCH volume 2). Among the local militia officers was Captain Nanfan of Hanley Castle. The militia system fell into disuse after 1715, but a new Worcestershire militia regiment was raised in 1770 under Colonel Nicholas Lechmere of Ludford Park in Shropshire, the owner of Cowley Park. Other militia officers included Captain Cresswell of Jamaica Farm in Howsell (1780s). Nicholas Lechmere Charlton resigned as colonel of the militia in 1795.

4 The Township of Great Malvern

Sir Bromley Bromley of Holt in Worcestershire was lord of the manor of Great Malvern in 1600. However the grandest house in the town belonged to the Savage family of Elmley Castle, the Jacobean style Abbey House on the site of the present Abbey Hotel. Anne Savage 'widow of Great Malvern', the daughter of John Knotsford (purchaser of the former monastic precinct and home farm in the 1540s) died in 1625. The Bromleys of Holt sold the manor of Great Malvern to the Foley family in 1741. The Foleys later resided at Stoke Edith in Herefordshire. The former monastic church of Greast Malvern Priory had been purchased by the parish in 1540.

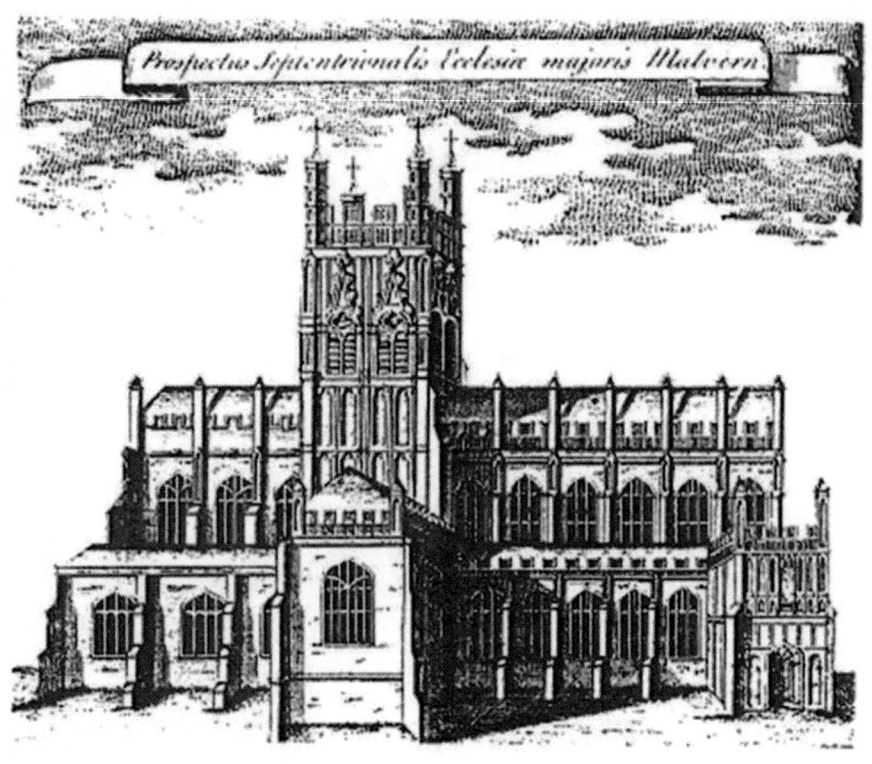

Great Malvern Priory church in 1725

The parish church was served by a vicar, employed by the owners of the rectory (or vicarage) who was paid a small salary, supplemented by the 'small tithes' of the parish. The income from the 'great tithes' (the cereal crops) went elsewhere, for example in 1714 they were paid to the rector of Madresfield (see list of tithes in Nott). The bells in the tower were added to in 1611 by two bells, one paid for by "I.H." and "E.H." (perhaps the Hornyold family of Blackmore Park, although they were Catholics) the second by I.H. and E.H. and Ann and John Savage, with three more bells added in 1706-7.

In 1722 the old wooden pews in the church were removed and replaced under the supervision of the churchwardens, with the permission of the Rev. William Byrche chancellor of the diocese of Worcester (and father of Thomas Byrche Savage the later owner of Abbey House). All the parishioners were allocated specific seats in the new pews, in a list that survives at Worcester Record Office. The list begins with the names of nine 'particular houses':

- Madm. Savage's House
- Mr. Thornburgh's
- Mr. Pooles's
- Mr. Dowdeswell's
- Mr. Gifford's de Mott
- Mr. Skelton's
- The vicar's wife &c
- Richard Turner's
- The Exciseman's family

It continues with properties in Malvern Town, and then out into the country including 'Link End' and 'Baldenhall Green' as discussed in later chapters.

Madm. Margaret Savage of Abbey House died in the same year, and was perhaps the last of the family to reside in Great Malvern, the principal family house was in Elmley Castle. Mr. John Thornburgh's house was in Barnards Green (see below) and Mr. Rowland Gifford owned the Moat Court estate.

Mr. Dowdeswell was clearly a wealthy man, but the location of his house is not identified. He was probably a junior member of the Dowdeswell family of Pull Court in Bushley. A George Dowdeswell (with the family coat of arms) was involved in a property transaction in Great Malvern in 30&31st Ch II (c.1679, Worcestershire Fines) and had the lease of the manor of Wichenford in 1695 (National Archives). Brian Smith records that George Dowdeswell gave £75 (in his will) in 1711 for bread for the poor of the parish.

The list of pews for Malvern Town includes the house of John Lutwich (parish clerk and school-master) and names four inns: the Talbot, the Crown, the Angel, and the Red Lion. The Unicorn, often reckoned the oldest inn in Great Malvern is not listed, although the building is shown on the map of 1744 (plot #448 below). The assumption is that either the Talbot or the Angel was renamed as the Unicorn at a later date, noting that the unicorn was a heraldic supporter of the arms of Henry Bromley when created Lord Montfort in 1741.

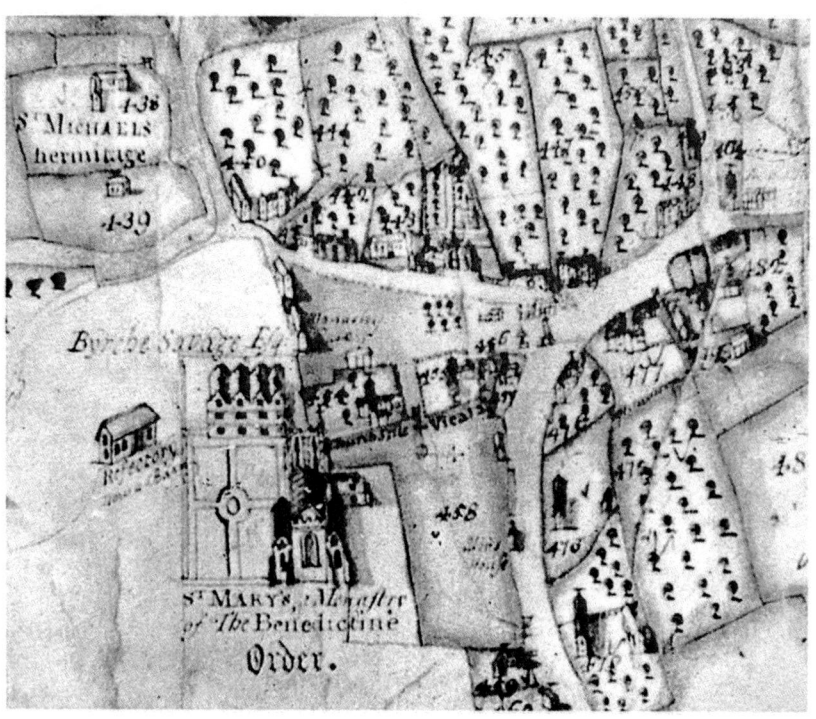

Detail of the map of 1744 (glass slide at Malvern Museum)

A small portion of the Foley estate map of 1744 is shown above, covering the centre of Great Malvern with west at top. To the west and north of the church is the triangular marketplace, adjoining the main road from Worcester to Ledbury and with a market cross shown at the northern corner, at the top of the modern Church Street. West and south of the church is Abbey House belonging to Byrche Savage Esq. and the 'Refectory', the 'Guesten Hall' of the medieval priory, since used as a barn. Post-medieval alms houses are shown at the edge of the churchyard (#458) on Church Street.

In the 18th century it became fashionable to take the water at Malvern Wells on the site of the Holywell. Dr. John Wall of Worcester had publicised the virtues of the purity of Malvern water starting in 1743, and a spa house and bath house were in existence in 1757 (see Weaver) with accommodation available locally and also at Abbey House in Great Malvern kept by John Dugard, where Benjamin Stillingfleet stayed in 1757 (see Smith).

The popularity of taking the water in Great Malvern itself came later, early in the 19th century and is well documented elsewhere. It led to the rapid growth of the town with the Foley Arms Hotel, the Royal Library and Coburg Baths all complete by 1823. The famous 'Water Doctors' arrived in 1842.

5   Baldenhall, Barnards Green and Poolbrook

The hamlet of 'Baldenhall Green' (as defined in the list of pews) seems to have stretched along the present Guarlford Road, from Barnards Green as far as Guarlford Court. The name 'Barnards Green' is not used either in the list of pews of 1722, or on the Foley estate map of 1744. Instead we have 'Crownhill' in 1722 and 'Merry Vale' in 1744 (on the site of the modern roundabout and shopping centre). The name 'Barnets Green' is shown on the map of 1744, but in front of the current Barnards Green House. The name Barnards Green first appears on slightly later maps, notably on Isaac Taylor's map of Worcestershire of 1772 (see 'Portrait of Malvern') and on Cary's map of 1787. The modern Court Road was known as 'Pullen' Street in 1722, and Hall Green appears as 'Hailend' and 'Leonards End'.

Most of the property in Baldenhall was owned by the manor of Great Malvern, and either farmed by tenants (as at Court Farm) or held by copyhold from the manor. Court Farm is shown as plot number 1 on the 1744 map and was probably the site of the manorial courts. In 1722 it is listed as 'Mr Bromley's Farm' on Pullen Street, with tenant William Young.

There had been an earlier (and quite separate manor) named 'Porters' at Baldenhall in the mid-16th century, owned by the Burghill family. This was possibly later the freehold property known as Pigeon House Farm, owned in 1744 by Henry Giles gent. He was obviously a wealthy man and maybe even the Henry Giles who was mayor of Worcester in 1701 (and a clothier). Henry Giles gave £10 to the parish of Great Malvern, a gift confirmed by his son, Thomas Giles in January 1746. A later owner of Pigeon House farm was John Williams, whose name has been added to the 1744 map at a later date.

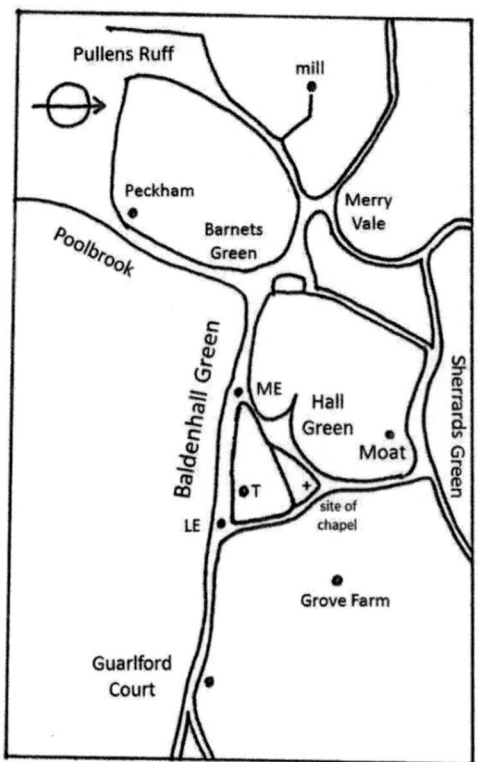

We can begin to understand the structure of the pews list and the location of the farms and homes of the pew holders, by comparing the list with the Foley estate map.

The sketch map shows the basic road network around 'Baldenhall Green' in 1744, traced from the estate map and with selected names (both ancient and modern) added. Note that west is at the top. On the sketch: T is the tithe house, LE is the Lower Elm and ME is the Middle Elm.

Sketch map of Baldenhall and Barnards Green in 1744.

The pew for 'Mr. Wilson's tithe house' appears near the top of the list for 'Baldenhall Green' and is also shown on the map of 1744, as is 'John Saunders' freehold' (Francis Saunders in 1744). This suggests that we should proceed westwards along the road as we read down the list of pews. Brian Smith records that the tithe barn, shown in 1744 close to the Friar's Elm was where the overseers of the poor distributed a bread charity, and that the site of the medieval St Leonard's chapel was nearby (as marked on the map).

The Middle Elm in the mid-19th century (from Lees)

It is instructive to plot the outline of the Foley estate's farms in 1831 onto the map of 1744. East of the Lower Elm in 1831 (i.e. towards Guarlford) was the farm of Mr. George Need (now New House Farm in Guarlford) but with adjoining lands at Woodbridge (in Malvern) marked as 'Thomas Need freehold' in 1744. Beyond the Lower Elm, to the north and east of Need's farm was the large Grove Estate, farmed by Mr. Joseph Bosworth in 1831 (also now in Guarlford). In the 18th century the parish of Great Malvern stretched through Guarlford and as far as Clevelode, but these are not part of modern Malvern and so are not covered in detail in this book.

South of the Lower Elm in 1831 was the Lower Elm estate, farmed by Mrs. Hannah Elia. "Workhouse, orchards and yard" are marked, by the Lower Elm itself. The farmhouse of "Late Hart's" Farm was on Hall Green, presumably the 'Hartland' Farm listed in 1722, and occupied in 1831 by Mr. Richard Banford. In 1831, the farm was in two large sections, split by the Moat Farm estate, with more farm buildings on Sherrards Green. This section is now Sherrards Green Farm and the buildings are in Guarlford.

Moving westwards along the main road from the Lower Elm to the Middle Elm, there was freehold land to the north in 1744 (including the tithe barn and the land of Francis Saunders) and this was Rose Farm owned by Samuel Roe in 1840/41 (see 'The Guarlford Story'). To the south of the road in 1831 was the farm of William Bullock, and then the fields of Barnards Green Farm occupied by Mr John Beard, with his farm buildings opposite the Middle Elm.

Continuing westwards, the smallholding of Captain Cullis was followed by Mill Farm on the south side of the road, occupied by Mr. Isaac Roberts in 1831, and with a patchwork of fields and cottages to the north, the fields belonging variously to Barnards Green Farm, to Little Nurden Farm and to John Probert's farm. This brings us to the cottages on 'Barnets Green' in 1744.

Turning south along Poolbrook, beyond the cottages at the corner was Pool Brook Farm, occupied by Mr. Richard Greenaway in 1831, followed by further cottages. Returning along the western side of Poolbrook, Miss Dandridge owned freehold property including the house called Peckham in 1831 (John

Baylis in 1744), with the 'Reddings' fields of Pool Brook Farm behind. After the fields of Mr. Williams (part of Pigeon House Farm in 1831) came Barnards Green House, leased by Miss Dandridge from the Foleys. Her father John Dandridge of the City of Worcester gentleman was involved with business in Malvern as early as 1750 dealing with John Warner of Great Malvern, tanner over two pieces of ground called 'Pool Furlongs' (Herefordshire Record Office). John Dandridge had moved to Malvern by 1764 being resident at 'Baldens Green' in 1778. His daughters were dealing with the estate by 1789.

The geography from 'Barnets Green' to 'Merry Vale' is complicated, so a sketch map is useful, based on the Foley estate map of 1744. The list of pews from 1722 moves from Baldenhall Green, to Pool Brook, to Crownhill and then to Pullen Street. The property known as Crownhill in 1831 is shown on the sketch, the leasehold of Thomas McCann. Thomas Cother had a property in the area known as Crownhill in 1722 and also appears on the 1744 map.

Sketch map of Barnards Green in 1744

Also listed under Crownhill in 1722 were Madm. Nanfan at 'Burnt House' (perhaps Barnards Green House) and Mr. Thornburgh who had an important residence somewhere in Malvern, appearing at the top of the pews listing.

It is possible that Madm. Nanfan was the widow of Captain Thomas Nanfan of the Worcestershire militia, who had a number of disputes with the Langston family over properties in Hanley Castle and Malvern. Thomas was a junior member of the Nanfans of Birtsmorton, and appears on their pedigree in the Herald Visitation of Worcestershire of 1683 with a son aged 14, which would put his widow, Madm. Nanfan in her seventies in 1722.

The will of Mr. John Thornburgh of St John's in Bedwardine (1728) lists a number of properties in Suckley, Alfrick and Knightwick and three properties in Malvern: a messuage, tenement, garden and orchard at 'Bernerds Green' in the parish of Malvern, a freehold estate called 'Moars Barns' in the parish of Malvern in the possession of John Silvester, and also a copyhold estate in Great Malvern, also in the occupation of John Silvester. The family of Thornborough of Suckley appears in the Heralds Visitation of 1683 showing a John Thornborough aged 11 (and so 56 in 1728) and probably our man since his mother's maiden name was Ross which fits with his cousin in the will.

The final entry for Crown Hill in 1722 is for John Warner, and the next entry (under Pullen Street) is for Mr. Bromley's farm (i.e. Court Farm) which may have been the adjacent property. The list for Pullen Street also includes the mill of John Bellars (on Clarence Road).

The present centre of Barnards Green (roundabout and shops) was named Merry Vale in 1744. The name appears once more in the will of William Williams in 1780. Mr. Williams was a former steward of the Lygons of Madresfield and by 1780 he owned what was later known as Pigeon House Farm, a dovecote is mentioned in the will. The name Merry Vale may be medieval in origin, derived from the Saxon 'maere' (a boundary) or may possibly refer to the merry, a type of black cherry (there were a number of cherry orchards in the parish) although there is another Merry Vale in the city of Worcester, where cherries are unlikely.

In 1831 the land to the west of Merry Vale was Downes Farm occupied by Mr Valentine Ridler and to the north were the farm buildings of Mr. William Young (later Lydes Farm) who had fields on Fiddlers Pit Lane (the modern Madresfield Road). Behind the farm buildings were two fields owned by Mr. Benjamin Johnson esq. in 1744, now the site of Great Malvern Cemetery.

The document listing the allocation of pews in 1722 concludes with the signatures of the two 'old' church wardens: Joseph Baylis and John Bellars. The Baylis family owned a considerable amount of freehold property in Malvern in 1744 including a Mr. John Baylis 'of Ledbury' to the south of Mr. Savage's main estate, Mr. John Baylis at Peckham, and Mr. Baylis at Pickersley Farm (as detailed below), while John Bellars had the 'upper' manorial mill in 1714 (tithe listing – see Nott) and in 1722, and a later John Bellars was at Pickersley Farm before 1800. John Powell had the 'lower' mill in 1714, by Mill Farm.

To the north and east of Barnards Green is Moat Court. Rowland Gifford purchased the Moat Court estate for £272 in 1605. Another Rowland Gifford appears in the list of pews in 1722, and Mr (John) Gifford is shown on the map in 1744. John Gifford, gent died in 1789 (PCC wills) when Joseph Williams 'of Moat Court' was executor of his estate.

6   Malvern Link

This chapter considers the hamlets, farms, mills, houses and families around Link Common, in the two parishes of Great Malvern and Leigh.

South of the Link - Great Malvern

Running westwards along the southern edge of the Link towards the Hills, the major properties shown on the Foley estate maps of 1831 were:

- Northend farm: then called 'Nurden' farm, a Foley property
- Pickersley farm: owned by John Bellers jun.

- Link End Farm: a Foley Property
- Cockshot Farm
- The Lodge

Northend Farm was farmed by Thomas Saunders in 1722. Almost a hundred years earlier in 1626, Richard Morton of the Gritt in Upper Howsell named William Knight of Northende in the parish of Malvern as one of the overseers of his will, and William Knight's will of 1657 shows that he had a mixture of freehold, leasehold and copyhold property in the area (although his tenancy of Northend Farm is not mentioned). The farmer at Nurden Farm in 1831 was Miss M Bullock.

The 1722 pew list records that the farmer at Pickersley Farm was Francis Warner (an old Malvern family name). The owner of the farm is not clear, but the Foley estate map of 1744 names Mr Baylis. By 1831 Pickersley Farm was owned by John Bellars junior. The Worcester Quarter Sessions records record that at Easter 1802, John Bellers junior of Great Malvern, 'mealman' (i.e. miller) and Surveyor (of the parish) reported on the progress of highway repairs. John Bellars of Pickersley died in 1848 aged 84, according to his tomb-stone in the priory churchyard.

The map of the Chase of 1633 shows the freehold property of Thomas Winsmore in this area, making it possible that he was an earlier owner of Pickersley Farm. The Winsmores were a prominent family in Leigh in the 16th and 17th centuries: a Thomas Winesmore was the constable of Leigh in 1634, and William Winsmore (died 1656, and a servant of Leicester Devereux Viscount Hereford) had the lease of Hill Mill near Leigh Sinton. The militia assessment of 1641 lists Francis Reade and Richard Reade in Malverne Magna, apparently wealthy farmers, and the will of Francis Reade (d.1655) at the National Archives confirms that he had the lease of 'Pickersly' in 1646 when he wrote the will. A footnote in the Victoria County History (n28) records that in 1701 Pickersleigh Farm had belonged to the Haynes family.

A Victorian photograph Pickersleigh Court (Brian Iles collection)

Link End Farm was part of the Foley estates in 1831. The tenant at Linkend Farm in 1722 was the Widow Bowen. Later in the century a George Rance was the farmer at the Link, according to his gravestone in the Priory churchyard, dated 1788 (his son William, also farmer at the Link has the neighbouring headstone). The farmer in 1831 was John Mason.

The Cockshot estate had been purchased by Sir George Strode, and was given by him to the church of St James in Clerkenwell in London in 1657 to support a charity. Sir George Strode was the owner of the third of the Chase which had been enclosed for the Crown, the process starting in the 1630s and finally completed in 1664 by his son Nicholas Strode. Cockshot Farm was not part of the Chase, although purchased from Sir Cornelius Vermuyden (when the tenant of 'Cockshute' was John Coleman) who had presumably acquired it in or around 1630. The farmer in 1722 was Edward Shaw,

The Lodge: the land shown on the 1831 estate map west of the Worcester Road was perhaps the leasehold property of Thomas Wylde (of the Commandery in Worcester?) named on the pews list in 1722. The house named 'The Lodge' appears to have been built after the date of the Foley estate map of 1744. It is shown on Mary Southall's perspective plan of Great Malvern (c.1820) as the property of Mr. John Surman (and the temporary residence of the Dean of Worcester). Mr. Surman is shown as the leaseholder on the 1831 estate map, when the house had "kitchen and pleasure gardens, lawns, plantations, shrubbery and cherry orchard".

The modern Malvern Link Common is what remains of that part of Link Common which lay in the parish of Great Malvern. All of the the Link Common in the parish of Leigh was enclosed in the late 1770s. Even in Malvern, parts of the Common have been lost due to encroachments, particularly in the Link Top area where the properties of Philip Ballard and of William Wall Esq. are shown on the Foley estate maps of 1831, west of the modern Graham Road, along with the parish workhouse on Worcester Road. Further west there were further encroachments at 'Oak Orchard', along the present Cowleigh Road.

North of the Link – Howsell in Leigh

The medieval moated manor house at Cowley sat on the (then) parish boundary between Leigh and Cradley. The manor was purchased by Rowland Berkeley a prominent Worcester clothier in 1604, and subsequently sold to Sir Walter Devereux, who received license to create a small deer-park there in 1625. The manor house was probably destroyed in the Civil War, and the manor and park was sold to the Lechmere family of Severn End later in the century (by 1674 – Worcestershire Fines). Anthony Lechmere, the grandson of Judge Sir Nicholas Lechmere (d.1701) is recorded as selling timber from Cowley Park in 1709, apparently for pit-props for use in mines in the Forest of Dean (catalogue of Herefordshire Record Office).

The tything of Howsell in the parish of Leigh is now part of Malvern. Along its southern edge it included several hundred acres of the Link, part of Malvern Chase, and to the north a number of large farms, some belonging to the lords of the manor and farmed by tenants, but others freehold from an early date.

Three parcels of the Link were enclosed for the Crown when the Chase was disafforested in the 1630s, these became Brick Farm, Jamaica Farm and Moors Farm, purchased by the Hornyold family of Blackmore Park in 1768. The rest of the Link in the parish of Leigh was granted to Sir Walter Devereux and only enclosed after the Parliamentary Act of Inclosure at the end of the 1770s. This included common land as far north as the present Dyson Perrins School.

Farms owned by the lords of the manor, the Somers-Cocks family of Eastnor Castle in the late 1830s (tithe apportionment) included Cross Farm and Link Lower House Farm on the Leigh Sinton Road, and Great Buckmans Farm and Howsell Farm (later Elms Farm) on the Lower Howsell Road. Upper Howsell also had a number of large freehold properties, including Cales Farm, Pale Farm and Gritt Farm, all with histories stretching back before 1600.

Cales Farm, adjoining Cowley Park Farm is recorded as early as 1486, when it belonged to Pershore Abbey ('survey' at the National Archives). In 1558 it was among the possessions of the former abbey bailiff of Leigh, William Collys as listed in his will, and so later became part of the Colles family's manor of Leigh, sold to Walter Devereux in 1615. The will of James Morton (1666) states that he had a lease of the messuage, toft, land meadow and pasture called Callis (or Calles) and also the nine acres of Cowley farm that lay amongst the land called Callis. By the time of the rent rolls of the manor of Leigh from the 1740s, (Worcester Record Office) Cales Farm was a freehold property owned by Mr. John Garway, who had acquired the farm under the will of his great-uncle Caleb Rudolph, a Ledbury merchant who had owned the farm as early as 1734. The freehold may date from the 1670s.

In the mid-17th century, Leicester Devereux Viscount Devereux made a number of agreements relating to local properties including with James Morton of Leigh Sinton (1653), with Richard Morton of the Gritt (1661-62, see below) and with Edward Kinge of Leigh, gent regarding a messuage and toft called 'Callis' (1675/6). This seems to have been the point when Cales Farm was separated from the manor becoming a freehold property.

Pale Farm, next to Cales Farm was owned by Francis Morton in 1714 (his memorial slab is in Great Malvern Priory church) who claimed descent from Sir Rowland Morton, 'remembrancer' to King Henry 8th. During the mid-17th century the farm seems to have been in the possession of three brothers, Humphrey (who also had property in Eastnor and Ledbury and gave the farm named 'Pales' in Leigh to his son Francis in his will (1670, Herefordshire VCH wills project)), William (compounded in 1655) and James (d.1666 when living at the old manor house in Leigh Sinton) perhaps all sons of John Morton. The Great Malvern parish register of 1608 refers to "John Morton's house at the Lynkesyde", and the court rolls for the manor of Leigh have a John Morton "de le Lynke" (1593/4). It is quite possible that the name Pale Farm came from its position on the edge of the Chase (i.e. on the fence or 'pale'), rather than on the boundary of Cowley Park (as suggested by Brian Smith) which was two farms away. In the mid-18th century (1744) Pale Farm was owned by another Francis Morton, nephew of Francis and husband of Elizabeth Cliffe of Mathon (married in 1722). The Pale was owned by Mr. William Dowding in 1781 (Land Tax Returns) and later by his son Charles Dowding.

Gritt Farm was associated with a quite separate family also named Morton. A William Morton appears in the court roll of 1525 in association with Francis Folyotte (of Pirton), the owner of the Gritt – as established in the court of chancery c.1510 (National Archives). The will of Richard Morton of 1591 is held by the Worcester Record Office, and the Leigh Parish Registers record the burial of Joana Morton 'of Greete', his widow in 1604. The ownership of the Gritt passed from the Folliott family to Sir William Courten of London in 1624, when they sold their Pirton estates. Courten's daughter Anne married Essex Devereux, the eldest son of Sir Walter Devereux of Leigh Court in 1634, and this seems to be the route by which the Gritt became a property of the manor. Essex Devereux drowned in the Teme without heirs, and so it was his brother Leicester Devereux who succeeded to the manor of Leigh.

The will of Richard Morton of the Greet (1674) records that the Greet had been purchased from (Leicester Devereux) Viscount Hereford for the sum of £320 in 1662, by Richard, his brothers John and Thomas and his brother-in-law James Morton (of Leigh Sinton) for the benefit of Richard Morton and his heirs. The surviving brick farmhouse at the Gritt was built in 1719 by Richard's grandson John Morton.

Two smaller freehold properties in Upper Howsell are worthy of note, Tanhouse farm owned by the Baxters in the 17th century, and the approximately 30 acres of freehold property of Joseph Pennel sold to the church of Great Malvern in 1743. The terrier, bound-up within the Great Malvern parish registers clearly defines the property including outlying strips in the common fields, and the names the neighbouring farmers including John Page 'tanner' and John Morton of the' Grett' gentleman. Rent from these lands was used to help support the vicar of Great Malvern, and they were identified as the 'Church Glebe Lands' on the tithe map.

A number of common fields in Upper Howsell can be identified in this terrier, in the Parliamentary Act of Inclosure (1776) and in local wills. These include the Cother fields, Mosset and Halfkey to the west of the Leigh Sinton Road and 'Intailfield' (Interfield), Mensfield and Hadfield to the east.

The later Halfkey Farm was a product of Inclosure, but in the manorial record of 1747 is the following: £5 "of John Pudge for a fine to adding two lives in a Copyhold estate called Halfkey in Leigh", a payment extending the family's tenure of their smallholding, presumably now Pudges Farm.

Properties in Lower Howsell included Jamaica Farm and Moors Farm, both enclosed from the Link Common and belonging to the Hornyold family after 1768. Beyond the end of the former common, marked by the Link Elm were Townsend Farm (with farm buildings at the corner of Spring Lane, shown as 'Nicholas Lane' on the map of 1633) and Link Mill. In the mid-19th century Townsend Farm was owned by the Madresfield estate and farmed by Mr. James Bellers (trade directories). The building at Link Mill is shown on the Foley estate map of 1744, and the mill is mentioned in the will of Wiiliam Stoakes of Cradley, gent of 1711 (National Archives).

"To Sarah Woodyatt daughter of Richard Woodyatt late of Cradley deceased all that meadow called Mill Meadow and Mill Ground Piece containing about 6 acres lying between the lands of the said William Stoakes on the east and west sides thereof, a common field called Bradley Field on the north side and the highway leading from Malvern to Worcester on the south."

A number of properties in Lower Howsell were purchased by William's father at the end of the 17th century. Sarah Woodyatt married John Morton of Gritt Farm in 1712, and in the court roll of the manor of Leigh of 1744/45 Mr John Morton of the Gritt is recorded as paying 2s-6d rent for the freehold property called 'Powell's Mill' (Worcester Record Office).

The Rental Rolls of the 1740s and the Land Tax Returns of the second half of the 18th century are useful tools in understanding the descent of the farms in Upper Howsell, and the changes after Parliamentary Inclosure in 1776. They identify farm names and owners and the names of farm tenants and smallholders. In the 1740s the 'Great Rents' were from Francis Woodyatt for 'Baxters' (£22) and "Ditto for Slops" (£12) and from Mr. William Gabb for 'Farnish Parkes' (near Halfkey, £2-10s). Francis Woodyatt was the principal tenant of the manor at Upper Howsell before 1781 and map evidence (a plan based on the Inclosure Map of 1776) places him at Link Lower House Farm and/or at Cross Farm. A number of farms were identified only by the names of their tenants, or former tenants. The 'Chief Rents issuing out of freeholds in Leigh' included "Mr. Davis apothecary for a freehold near Newlands Green" (now the Swan at Newland, £1) and the freehold farms at Cales, the Pale and the Gritt. Manorial payments included "Paid to John Hooper two bills for iron work done at Howsell and Sinton pounds" and "Paid Mr. Deakin a year's Land Tax for the tythes of Sinton and Howsell due at Lady Day 1748".

Land Tax was charged at the rate of two shillings in the pound (sometimes three shillings) based on the nominal value of farms and estates at the end of the 17th century. So, for example the rent of £22 for Baxters in the 1744 is reflected in a Land Tax of £2-8s for "late Bagsters" in 1767. Four separate Land Tax returns survive for Leigh before the complete set of assessments for Worcestershire begins in 1781 (Worcestershire Record Office). They are particularly helpful in identifying changes in farm names, so for example "late Stoaks's" (1764) a.k.a. Stokes Farm (1774) became Brick Farm in 1781. Mr. Richard Morton is at Gritt Farm and Mr. Page is at the Tanhouse (1767).

Elsewhere in Leigh, William Dowding owned Pipe Elm Farm (in Leigh Sinton) in 1771 but also Pale Farm in 1781, Mr. Richard Harris was the tenant at Buckmans in 1774 and Capt. Cresswell was the tenant at 'Jamaco' in 1781. A similar analysis of Land Tax Returns could be helpful for Lower Howsell and for farms in Great Malvern.

In the 18th century the drive towards more efficient arable farming in large compact farms, rather than communally cultivated open fields led to the enclosure of the countryside by the major landowners through Parliamentary 'Acts of Inclosure'. The smallholders and smaller tenant farmers often lost out during this process, losing long-standing customary rights, and this led to an increased dependence on the Poor Law system and the drift of the rural population to the cities, helping to fuel the Industrial Revolution.

The Link Common in Leigh had not previously been enclosed or ploughed and there was active opposition to the Act of Inclosure of 1776 in Upper Howsell and the Link, as recorded in a number of sources:

- "Hostility to the enclosure of the former Malvern Chase led local people to prevent John Andrews the surveyor, from marking out the enclosure boundaries" (Jeremy Black, "Historical Atlas of Britain").
- Thirteen people were charged with riot and Thomas Kemp of Leigh was sent to prison for six months (Roy Palmer, "Folklore of Worcestershire").
- In January 1778 "malicious and evil disposed persons ... did pull up and prostrate some posts and rails and quick (hedges) set up and planted on part of Link Common" and burnt them on the new enclosure made by Sir Charles Cocks, lord of the manor (Brian S Smith, "A history of Malvern", quoting from a contemporary account).
- In November rioters again assembled on the open part of the common and "with their faces blackened, and being otherwise disguised, and armed with guns and other offensive weapons, and in the most daring manner did cut down, burn and entirely destroy all the posts, gates and rails" (Ditto.).

- One of the men employed in fencing the new enclosures, Edward Gummery of Berrow was murdered with three of his family in 1780 in revenge for his innocent part in the affair (Brian S Smith).

So far there has been no mention of the hamlet of Malvern Link. Before 1800 there were no significant settlements in the area, only the farms and small clusters of cottages in Upper Howsell (at either end of Tanhouse Lane), along the Lower Howsell Road and on the Worcester Road, where the name Malvern Link is shown on the first edition OS map (surveyed in 1817). The map shows the turnpike road across the Link, with a toll house by the Link Mill. The history of the rapid growth of Malvern Link into a village and a town belongs to the 19th century, the church of St. Matthias in the Link was not founded until the 1840s (see Drake's book on Malvern Link).

Conclusions

This book has provided an introduction to the history of Malvern in the 17th and 18th centuries. At the Census of 1801, Great Malvern was still little more than a large village with a population of just 819, in 170 houses.

There are many records still to be explored, including property deeds, wills, parish registers, manorial records, inclosure awards, and hearth tax and land tax returns. The later tithe maps are also an invaluable resource for looking backwards into the 18th century and identifying farm and field names. In researching this book, much more of this detail has been investigated for Upper Howsell than for the parish of Great Malvern. Even for Upper Howsell, new records are coming to light, with the recent release of the Manorial Documents Register for Worcestershire, including the court rolls, rentals and estate maps (of 1781) for the manor of Leigh, archived at Eastnor Castle.

The local history of this period tends to be a neglected area, compared with (for example) the Water Cure and the Victorian Town, but a wealth of records are available for further study.

Appendix – Additional Information

A. Grazebrook's heraldry contains a number of appendices, providing some useful insight into the wealthiest of the local community, for example:

- Disclaimers list (heralds' visitation of 1634):
    - Nicholas Phelps, Much Malvern
    - Francis Ross, Malvern
- Fined for not taking knighthood at coronation of Charles I
    - William Cave of Leigh, £10
    - Francis Rosse of Gt. Malvern, £12
- Gentry to find horse (c.1660)
    - Lester Devereux, Viscount Hereford
    - William Langston*
    - Nicholas Lechmore esq.
- Landowners in 1703-4 (with freehold or copyhold lands worth £10 pa.)
    - John Warner tops the list as the wealthiest resident in Malverne Magna. Unfortunately the original list for Malvern is damaged, but (for example) in Leigh the list is topped by Edward Martin, gent of Leigh Court, and in Madresfield by William Lygon esq. Next on the list for Malvern are Richard Leeth and Nathanial B(arnes ?). Richard Leeth is also recorded in 17 Ch II (c. 1666, Worcestershire Fines) but the location of his property is unclear. Nathanial Barnes appears on the pew list of 1722 under "Cleeveload &c" which includes Guarlford.

Note *. William Langston appears in the main body of the book, in the family of 'Langstone of Sedgeberrow and Malvern' who are recorded as bearing arms in 1634, when the head of the family was his father Francis. The Langstons were in dispute with Captain Nanfan at the end of the century, over property in Hanley Castle and in Great Malvern (National Archives).

B. The Burghill family of 'Thinghill Parva' held the manor of 'Porters' in Baldenhall in the mid-16th century, but the descent of the estate is unclear. There is a memorial to John Burghill the lord of Little Thinghill in Withington

(Herefordshire) in the church of Broke in Norfolk, dated 1659. Grisell Burghill (presumably his widow) is recorded a number of times later in the century including in the Militia Assessments for Herefordshire of 1663 in Withington (assessed for £30).

Bibliography

- Victoria County History – Worcestershire (VCH). "A History of the County of Worcester" Volume 4 for Great Malvern and Leigh.
- Victoria County History – Worcestershire (VCH). "A History of the County of Worcester" Volume 2 for political, military and trade history.
- Brian S. Smith. "A History of Malvern". Second edition (1978).
- R. C. Gaut. "A History of Worcestershire Agriculture and Rural Evolution". (1939).
- Pitt. "General View of the Agriculture of the County of Worcester [1813]".
- Worcestershire County Records: Calendar of the Quarter Session Papers 1591-1643 (published 1900).
- Prerogative Court of Canterbury Wills, down-loadable via 'Documents On-line' at The National Archives website.
- Diocese of Worcester Wills at the Worcester Record Office.
- Hearth Tax and Land Tax records at the Worcester Record Office.
- Pamela Hurle. "The Forest and Chase of Malvern". Phillimore, (2007).
- Pamela Hurle and John Winsor. "Portrait of Malvern". (1985).
- Malcolm Atkin. "Worcestershire Under Arms". (2004).
- Grazebrook. "The Heraldry of Worcestershire", 2 volumes (1893).

- "An Index of Worcestershire Fines 1649-1714" (published 1896).
- Daphne Drake, "The Story of Malvern Link, Worcestershire".
- James Nott, "Church and Monastery of "Moche Malverne" (Great Malvern)". (1885).
- Cora Weaver, "The Holy Well at Malvern Wells". (2015).
- Edwin Lees, "The Forest and Chace of Malvern". (1877).
- The Guarlford History Group, "The Guarlford Story".
- Rev. W. Thomas. "Antiquitates Prioratus Majoris Malverne" (1725).
- Foley estate maps, 1831 (Malvern Museum).
- David Hope. "Great Malvern Priory's Historic Bells". Malvern Museum newsletter (September 2011).

Worcester token of 1788 commemorating the visit of King George III to the Three Choirs' Festival

An unusual view of the gatehouse taken from a wider view of Great Malvern Priory church in Nash's "Collections for the History of Worcestershire" (1799)